The Gun and the Scythe:
Poetry by an Army Ranger

by Luke Ryan

Copyright © 2019 by Luke Ryan
All rights reserved. No part of this book may be reproduced or used in any manner without the written permission of the copyright owner except for the use of quotations in a book review.

Dedicated to Patrick Hawkins, Cody Patterson, Jennifer Moreno, and Joseph Peters

Forward by the author:

The first time I ever heard shots fired in anger, I was a child to aid workers living in northern Pakistan. The first time those shots were intended for me, I was in eighth grade hiding under a library desk during the Murree Christian School shooting in 2002. Later, I would join the U.S. Army, become a Ranger with the 3rd Ranger Battalion and go on four deployments to Afghanistan. There, I became familiar with violence as a trained adult, in contrast to my experience as a child.

What did I discover about the nature of war and human conflict? It's an eternal thing, as basic to human nature as eating food, as physical as sex, and as spiritual as prayer. It doesn't happen in dark places, it makes places dark – a reoccurring image I realized had found its way into my poetry only after I had written it. It's not some hazy, mysterious disease you catch while in a combat zone, forcing you into madness as many modern films or books depict. It's also not a place where the obvious protagonists triumph in brazen victory over the evil devils, as many older films or books depict.

It's a place where the worst of humanity is shoved in your face and revealed to exist in your own heart as well as the hearts of everyone else. It's also a place where you witness firsthand human beings stand up against those horrifying things. It's a place of contrast – of shining light and terrible dark, of shattering grief and profound fulfillment.

The elements found in a war can be understood by anyone. Grief, courage, selflessness, brotherhood – these are not exclusive to the battlefield. However, in the midst of combat, they seem to be boiled down to their purest form, for better or worse.

Veteran or not, I hope you resonate with these words.

Regulars

Who is he?
He who scars the earth
He who pushes back against the venom
Or helps it on its way.

He is just a man in distant place
Who knows where to put his hands,
Where to put his feet,
And what might happen when he does.

No armor of silver
No heart of royalty
No body of stone
A mind like any other mind.

A chest rack plastered in dirt
A heart, red and fragile
A body, tired and broken
A mind, as precious as a mind can be.

He is just a man in distant place

Who knows where to put his hands,

Where to put his feet,

And what might happen when he does.

The Hooded Figure

Hello,

I'm here to take you away.

Do you see that field? Those mountains? The clouds that hang above?

We will go beyond those things.

Your cheeks are red. Redder than I imagined when I received the word to take you across the river.

When I see you, I see a train I once visited long ago

To take many men, women, and children.

The train was a spectacle—

It had been constructed with devotion

Admired with wonder and awe.

It powered forward on its maiden voyage,

On the crest of steaming to faraway places,

To drink in the sights of your green and blue marvel.

But the train slipped when it reached its cruising speed,

Derailed only moments after leaving the station.

Tragedy is my business, and business is always booming.
But I am an infinite being
And alongside my infinite devotion for crossing the river
I hold an infinite sorrow in the place you call your heart,
And I lament the future that has been painted in crimson on the wall behind you.

Yes, you may weep.
Weep, for you were a better man than those who will remain in this place for a hundred years.
Weep, for your dreams sprang and shone like a pure spring, and they were stolen from you.
Weep, for you never found the love you sought,
You never saw the children you wished so dearly to hold,
And you never had the privilege of wrinkles on your face,
Though I can see that you have miles on your shoes.

It's okay, you may let go of your rifle.
Here, take my staff, if you must grasp something.

Fear not,
This place is but a warm breath in the winter winds,
And we will carry onward.
There is a cabin I know of
With a warm fire and a soft pillow.

We will go there together
And wait for the others.

IED

A flash, an eruption of red in a sea of black.
No sound, not for my ears.
Only a flash.
Heat passes through me,
Like a campfire over and over
Passing through every inch of my flesh,
Through my brain and my gut.

The flash subsides.
My legs still carry my body,
My arms still carry my rifle.
I can see.
That's all I need to know.

Right then, let's get on with it.
There will be time to think later.

An Ancient Place with Ancient Blood

The snow falls gently
Dipping in the pools of red.
The Afghan mountainside:
Barren. Alone.

The noise has thundered away,
And the silence rolls back in
Filling the vacuum, along with a distant wind
Lonely and cold.

Just minutes ago,
This place was full of malice and terror
And the cries of a life as it burned its last few sparks
Now they all lay still among the rocks.

This is a quiet place,
An ancient place,
With ancient blood
On quiet rocks.

The Blazing Optimist

There is no time for pessimism in a firefight.
You fight until you win or you die,
And so it is off the battlefield as well.

The Taking

It was not a definitive ten seconds,
Where the world froze on its axis.
There was not an arc that led to that climax,
And my thoughts were not on the essence of
violence nor the nature of mankind.

It was a quick moment
Amidst a flurry of other quick moments.
I did what I knew
And crested the next corner.

These moments lay in obscurity.
Sometimes I call upon them,
Sometimes they call upon themselves.

Bard

Write it all down, he told me.
Take it from your heart and put it in your mind;
Take it from your mind and put it in your hands;
Take it from your hands and put it on the page.

One day you'll take it off the page,
And it will guide your hands;
It will ease your mind;
It will still your heart.

Hard Surfaces

Laughter echoes little
When you laugh among the pillows,
Under mountains of fleece,
And the walls made of paper.

Laughter echoes much
When it echoes through the arctic caves.
Across hard floors and vast, vacant spaces.
Even if it is through gritted teeth, it echoes much.

And it echoes all the louder
When other voices join the first
Among hard surfaces.

The Dark River

I am floating on a dark river
Sometimes it rages
Sometimes it's smooth
Always it flows.

When it rages, I can hoist the sails
Or drop them as the wind implores.
I can fight against the rain and wind,
Dodging the rocks and circumventing the deadly shore.

But when it's smooth—please, God, let it not be smooth—
When the current gently rocks,
Beseeching my mind on and on
Like a slow, unstoppable tidal wave,
It turns to a whirlpool of despair.

Ebbing slowly,

As it ebbs boulders into pebbles.

The hollow current

And the empty waves

Eroding consciousness,

But without discerning, and without cause.

Swirling, swirling, swirling.

The Military Working Dog

How can I thank you?
When you never had a choice?

And yet I do.
Every day I ponder the life
Of a creature who traded places with me
On the stairway to the eternal.

What does it say about me?
To be so inspired by a beast?
Or what does it say about a beast?
That he should so inspire the hearts of men?

Such combinations!
Of loyalty and love,
Grace and bravery,
Strength and innocence.

Should that such combinations exist within my own heart
But I am merely a man,
Clumsy and corrupt.
Not like you, unsullied with the nonsense of men.

How can I thank you?
When you never had a choice?

I don't know what to think about that
I don't know how to think about that
But my gratefulness will endure
For as long as my corrupt heart will beat.

The Way of the Ice

The ice has a way
Of freezing in your thoughts
Solidifying,
Lingering.

When you step outside and you see your breath
The ice comes back,
Weaving its frozen fingers
Through the annals of your memory.

When it thrashes your skin
And numbs your fingertips,
The ice comes back
Reminding you of the mountains,
Of the shivering and the stuttering,
Of the cold steel between your fingers and the wind biting your face.

Go back to the fireplace,
But let the ice remain in the back corner of your thoughts
Let it be a reminder
Of when misery bit you so.

Pack and Unpack

Fear?

Push it down.

Push it down below your ribs,

Down below the gut,

To a place where it cannot affect you.

Hate?

Push it down.

Past the hands of the enemy,

Past your eyes that see them work,

For you have an impartial job to do.

Hopelessness?

Push it down.

Past your scrambling feet,

Past your agitated voices,

For pessimism is best left for those off the battlefield.

Grief?

Push it down.

Past your eyes that fill with blood,

Past your own revolving heart,

For you must fight for the living.

These things are packed away now,

Like the shirts and socks and food at the bottom of your ruck.

But you've returned to base

And you must unpack.

These Things I Know

I know the softness of your skin
Because I know the roughness of the rocks.

I know the sweetness of your voice
Because I know the cries of a waning life in the night.

I know the warmth of your touch
Because I know the sting of ice and snow.

I know the safety of your embrace
Because I know the embrace of a wounded friend.

I know the stillness you bring my heart
Because I know the violence that lives within all hearts of all.

I know the flowers of your compassion
Because I know a place where such things did not bloom.

Animals and Angels

Rabid animals we,

Sunk to the levels of our ancestors

As will our children sink.

We erupt at the others,

Frantically biting at their necks,

Caged only by our primal bloodlust.

Clawing in a lightless night,

Dependent on whatever strength we muster

To power over others, to push them into oblivion.

~ ~ ~ ~

Brooding angels we,

Rising to the level of our ancestors

As will our children rise.

We carry the others,

Putting pressure on their precious necks,

Freed by our relentless pursuits.

Shining the small light,

Dependent on the angels to our flanks

To power over darkness and push it back for just another minute.

~ ~ ~ ~

All within a single soul.

No Parades

No parades for us
Just a crowd of silent shadows
Waiting on the tarmac.

No parades for us
At best a parade of one or two
A hug, a kiss, a handshake.

No parades for us
Equipment on the rack,
Uniforms in the locker.

No parades for us
Nor would we want them—
The praise of strangers.

We got what we wanted:
A cold beer on a soft couch
And the company of brothers.

I Have Been Many

Was that me among those mountains?
Brother to my left,
Muzzle flashes flickering to my front,
Rifle in my right.

Now I sit at my desk
Coffee to my left,
Monitor flickering to my front,
Mouse in my right.

Were these the same men?
Does the same mind govern the thoughts of
numbers and the thoughts of blood?
Do the same hands govern the striking of the keys
as they governed the striking of the hammer?

I have heard of the fog of war,
But I thought it crept and moved upon the
battlefield.
Now it moves around the corners of my mind,
Dividing what is from what once was.

Rage

The angriest people I have ever known
Have never fought in their lives.

The Value of Dirt

I peered up and saw a gentleman
Standing in his castle, directing and orchestrating.
He was a conductor of death, overseeing the crescendo of swords
From a very high place.

He pointed to the left,
And a legion extended with his finger.
He cried out to the right,
And a thousand ears turned to hear his voice.

We peered up at him, buried in a ceiling of clouds,
What kind of person could climb to such heights?
How many rungs was he required to grasp? How many walls was he required to scale?
Many smiled as they gaze above; many scowled.
All look upward.

All except for one fellow, standing behind me.
He bent to the earth and ground the particles of dirt into his palms.

"I pity the gentleman in the tower," he said,
"For he has never tasted dirt.
For all the rungs to his ladder, he has never grasped a spear.
And the only wall he has scaled, was a wall within the walls of the castle."

"How sorry I would be
Had I never been cut,
Never been mired in the mud,
Never been out of breath on a cold mountain.
How sorry I would be."

And I thought that I would like to be the fellow next to me,
In his tower which extended outward instead of up.
So I lowered my eyes to the dirt
And sought its comfort.

Combat is Simple

A bullet is fired
And the world goes away
The world of text shimmering on a screen
The world of horns and lights and digits and brights—
All snapped away, when the primer is struck.

Your purpose is clear:
Get around that corner.
Climb over that wall.
Fire through that window.

To a single goal, you offer it all up:
Your spirit, just to crest a single corner.
Your limbs, just to breech a single wall.
Your life, so the man to your side may not have to give his.

Your attention is not split
Between the numbers and the letters and the tiny hollow words.
It is not split
Between the cars and the money and the people in herds.

The words here are precious,
Necessary to act.
The actions here are precious,
Necessary to live.

It's a terrible business, fire and brimstone.
But it is simple
And that is something.

Fireworks

The dramatic battles of our lives
Takes minutes, seconds, milliseconds.

The rest is a culmination
Of small, hushed moments.

Dismiss those
And you dismiss the whole thing,
For the sake of a few fireworks.

Shoulder the World

The earth rests upon all our shoulders.
Can't you feel it?
It's strapped onto our backs,
The gravel digging and cutting,
And the oceans wet and clammy on our skin.

Some lay down,
Exhausted at the toil,
Grasping for water or some meager comfort.
And they lament that a planet should be so heavy.

Some roll to their sides,
Laughing at the thought of trying in the first place.
"Lifting is a pointless and perilous ordeal," the say.
"And all those who bear the burden are fools."

And some lift.
They struggle and stumble as they wrestle it higher.
They may collapse under its crushing weight,
Or they may muscle it up, from their knees to their feet.
But always they lift.

And whether they can shoulder the weight or not,
There are those who make sure it is elevated,
And those who make sure it is not.

Gold Star

A star of gold was stitched on her flag.
A brand, a mark, a eulogy, a tribute.
Honored to have given such life,
Crushed to have lost it.

Haunting echoes
Of a wailing mother on the airfield at Dover,
Desperately weeping
Into the quiet moments of the rest of my life.

Haunting echoes
Of a father made of titanium and steel
Reduced to a quivering pile
Of soft, soft tears.

Haunting echoes
In the shape of a lonely figure
Whose threads of life were once so intertwined,
Thrashed and burned and cut with jagged ends
Sobbing on the bathroom floor.

Haunting echoes
Are the sullen eyes of a child now aged
Desperately still,
Before a marker made of stone.

Those who bear that shimmering star
I embrace as my own.
A widow, my sister.
A parent, my heart.
And a child, my future.

The Medic

If he could take the very life out of his own bones,
And put it into his brother
Lying on the ground
Among the links and the shells,
Then he surely would.

But he cannot perform such miracles,
So he does what he can.
He runs through a downpour of bullets and the showering shrapnel
Which rip through the air and flesh with equal ease.

He has spent untold hours learning
Training. Preparing.
Untold hours;
Untold days;
Untold years of his life.
He does this for a task he hopes he will never use.

He pours those hours into his hands
So they know what to do when the moment comes.
And when that precious, terrible moment arrives,
He pours that training into his brother in need.
And as such
The medic pours his own life into the veins of his brother.

And if the time comes,
When his dear brother must pass
The medic holds his hand.
A mother was there when the soldier entered the world,
And try as he may, the medic could not keep him there
But rest assured he will be there when the soldier leaves.

A Marked Man

I am a marked man.
Marked to live,
Marked to suffer the loss,
Marked to fill my lungs,
While others are now empty and decayed.

I am a marked man.
Marked to remain wide-eyed,
Marked to suffer the sun,
Marked to remain awake,
While others sleep.

I am a marked man.
I don't regret the decisions made
And yet I lie awake in thought,
Would that I could
Trade my brother's mark for mine.

Repetition

He stands in front of a door.
The fire erupts, the door pulses backward.
The man in front of him enters, and he is close behind.
One goes right; the other goes left.

"Do it again!"

He stands in front of a door.
The fire erupts, the door pulses backward.
The man in front of him enters, and he is close behind.
One goes left; the other goes right.

"Do it again!"

His breath is heavy, and he hurries back,
He places the explosive on the door,
Position themselves,
Click-bang-enter.

"Do it again!"

As the sun goes down, the night vision goes up.
He steps into a sea of green and positions himself.
The fire erupts, the door pulses backward.
One goes right; the other goes left.

And again, and again, and again.

The Ship and the Heart

If I flew to the fiery core of the sun
I would fly but half of the distance yet traveled.
For the miles of a ship are naught
Compared to the miles of the heart.

And yet it's the miles of the ship
That put the miles on the heart.
And as the ship's gears turn
So they turn the gears of the heart.
As one ends, they both shall end.

48

Invisible Warriors

You can't see me.
You can't hear me.
I'm not a demon or a wraith,
I live at midnight and move through it silently,
Relentlessly toward you.
I am driven to upset your plans of mayhem.

I live in a world of emerald.
I bask in unseen light as I tread across the desert floor.
The stars are many,
Our lights are many,
Our signatures are few.

Invisible lines dance before me
And I see them all, though you cannot.
Your own compatriots move before me.
I see them all, though you cannot.

I hear the sounds of my kin

Coordinating

Pointing and gliding with deliberate precision.

Directing, ordering, attending to chaos.

But to you:

Silence. Darkness. Nothing.

Explorers Within

A warrior who dives into the depths of his own mind
Finds the brick that holds it upright,
Finds the mortar that sticks it together,
Understands the gears that turn.

A warrior who dives into the depths of his own heart
Knows from where the rivers flow,
Knows from where the anger rises,
Knows the weakness as well as strength.

A warrior who dives into the depths of his own soul
Understands the war that rages within,
Understands the effects of the war without,
Understands the why that drives us all.

The warrior who does not explore
Lives alone;
A stranger to his mind.
A stranger to his heart.
A stranger to his soul.

Creatures of Wanton Death

How recklessly we take the life of a mouse,
Scurrying in the corner,
Its consciousness overwhelmed with innocent fear,
Its tiny feet scurrying from the broom handle.
How recklessly we take the life of a mouse,
Whose crime was that it wanted to be warm.

How recklessly we take the life of a spider,
Dormant in the corner,
Because it does not have the pretty wings of a butterfly,
Its broken legs scurrying from the broom.
How recklessly we take the life of a spider,
Whose crime was that it built a home in a vacant corner.

"Surely we would never take a human life so recklessly,
Surely the takers of human life are a different breed
With scars on their faces and insides made of slime.
I value life!
As long as it is not disturbing, ugly, inconvenient, annoying, or in the way,
I value life,"
Said the one who did the killing
before the killing was done.

"Surely, I am not capable of pulling the trigger
On a crowd of unarmed faces or a child,
Or of changing a room full of air
Into a room full of gas.
I value life,"
Said the one who did the killing
Before the killing was done.

The Enemy

I have seen those
Who thirst for blood
Who inject themselves with rage
Addicts to bitterness and indignation.

They are given the chance
To strive for peace on the horizon,
And yet they prefer violent ends,
Laughing as the bridges burn.

For breakfast they feast on fury;
In the evening they dine on madness.
Their cruel thoughts don't always materialize as they hoped,
And yet they embrace cruelty like a friend.

I have seen those who proudly do not care
Of the wellbeing of others,
Who proudly do not care
If their neighbor chokes on his own blood.

I saw these things after the war,
When I came home
Where peace is a luxury
And rage a reasonable choice.
Or so they say.

Hills to Take

Remember the glory days? The days when there were hills to take and ropes to climb?
Remember when you had grit on your breath and purpose on your mind?
Remember it all?

You're not there.
You're here.

Remember when you pushed yourself to the limits of your potential?
Remember when you pushed yourself to the limits of your life?
Remember it all?

You're not there.
You're here.

Remember–

I do remember. I remember the things behind.
But what of the things ahead? Will there be any
hills to take or ropes to climb?

Yes.
But you can't climb a hill when you're busy looking
back at the last one.

Such Life Among Such Death

What are you doing this far out?
This is a place for those with strong backs and stronger legs,
A place where gunpowder sparks and thunder roars.
It is no place for one who cannot distinguish shapes from soldiers.

What will become of you?
Those who brought you here made a choice,
As did those I came with.
We all came to this place to meet with fire,
And here you lay,
Among the ashes in the furnace.

Why must you be here?
Are you not the thing for which we fight?
And yet we fight over the top of you,
Our boots come crashing down,
Smashing the road outstretched before you,
Fracturing the lens through which you see the world.

You have seen the blood of your father
And the blood of your mother,
Though you know not what red things are.
Why did they bring you here?
Knowing what fate would befall them?

Some questions cannot be answered.
Some things are just heavy.

Rest Easy, My Friend

My shift is over,
I passed on the torch so that better men may take my place
And better men took it.
They grappled with monsters so that I could take a knee.

And as I move forward, I look back
To those who remain on the line,
Paying a price I never paid
Though I have seen it paid before.

My shift is over
And now yours is over too.
Rest easy, my friend.
Others will pick up the torch where you left it.

There is an aching in my heart,
For those you love who have lost a piece of themselves,
The unique tapestry of a brilliant future
Stripped and burned by a cruel full stop.

But you need not worry about such things.
Yours is time to rest under the flag that rests on you.
Your brothers will take the torch, and they will see about your family.
Rest now.

Peace in the Dark

Where did I find peace?
Did I find it in the warm walls,
Away from the sting of the cold,
Under the blankets and next to the fire?

Did I find it in reprieve from thorns?
In the four walls of brick,
Where the shadows were kept outside
Away from my delicate flesh?

Did I find it where I was freed from worry?
Where the gold was plentiful,
Where food was on my table,
And the wine wasn't cheap?

I searched and I searched,
But peace was not there.

I found peace away from the warm walls
Away from the bricks and deep in the shadow.
Worried and gnawing and scratching and clawing,
Peace was buried in the ash and the trembling hands
of the undone.

Peace in a land where men wanted me dead,
But a few around me would not have it.
And peace most profound
When my life was offered upward.